JavaScript

Brian Evenson

Published by Wilson Publishers, 2023.

While every precaution has been taken in the preparation of this book, the publisher assumes no responsibility for errors or omissions, or for damages resulting from the use of the information contained herein.

JAVASCRIPT

First edition. March 6, 2023.

Written by Brian Evenson.

Introduction to JavaScript

JavaScript is an interpreted programming language, built on the EC-MAScript standard. The language definition is really broad since it can be defined as aprocedural language based on prototypes, imperative, weakly typed, and dynamic.

JavaScript is mainly used as a client side programming language implemented as part of a web browser to allow developers an improved way to implement user interface and dynamic features in web pages, although there are implementations of JavaScript on the server side (SSJS) the popularity of the language is due to the client side implementations alone.

JavaScript can also be found outside web applications, for example as a way to add interactivity to PDF documents and desktop widgets.

JavaScript was designed with a similar syntax as C, although it takes names and conventions from the Java programming language. However, despite the name Java and JavaScript are not related and have different semantics and purposes.

JavaScript was originally developed by Brendan Eich of Netscape under the name Mocha, which was later renamed to LiveScript, to finally being called JavaScript. The name change coincided approximately with the moment in which Netscape added support for Java technology in its web browser Netscape Navigator version 2.0B3 in late 1995. The name JavaScript was confusion, giving the impression that the language is an extension of Java, and it has been characterized by many as a marketing strategy for Netscape to gain prestige and innovate in what were the new web programming languages.

The following year Microsoft implemented a similar client side programming languages as part of its Internet Explorer 3.0 web browser. Microsoft called its client side language "jscript", to avoid problems related to the brand. The Jscript term seems so similar that the both "javascript" and "jscript" are often used interchangeably, but the specification of JScript is not 100% compatible with the ECMA specifications.

To avoid these incompatibilities, the World Wide Web Consortium (W3C) designed the standard Document Object Model (DOM, or document object model), which was incorporated in the version 6 of Internet Explorer and Netscape Navigator, Opera version 7, Mozilla Firefox since its first release, and all modern browsers thereafter.

In 1997 there was a proposal to submit JavaScript to the standard of the European Computer Manufacturers ' Association ECMA, which despite its name is not European but international, based in Geneva. In June 1997, it was adopted as an ECMA standard under the name of ECMAScript. JavaScript also became an ISO standard.

Because of its standardization and the great adoption of the internet, JavaScript has become the most used programming language in the planet.

Note: JavaScript is a registered trademark of Oracle Corporation. It is used under license by the products created by Netscape Communications and current entities such as the Mozilla Foundation.

Uses of JavaScript

JavaScript is present in most web pages today. Chances are that the page you are looking at right now contains the code for JavaScript. Try this activity: Right-click on a web page, then click 'View Source'. You should be able to find the word JavaScript somewhere in the code of the page.

While HTML markup language allows web developers to format content, JavaScript allows them to make the page dynamic. For example, HTML allows for making text bold, creating text boxes, and creating buttons, whereas JavaScript allows for changing text on the page, creating pop-up messages, and validating text in text boxes to make sure re q uired fields have been filled. JavaScript makes web pages more dynamic by allowing users to interact with web pages, click on elements, and change the pages.

What JavaScript can do for you

Let's take a step back and count the merits of JavaScript:

•JavaScript is very easy to implement. All you need to do is put your code in the HTML document and tell the browser that it is JavaScript.

•JavaScript works on web users' computers - even when they are offline!

••JavaScript allows you to create highly responsive interfaces that improve the user experience and provide dynamic functionality, without having to wait for the server to react and show another page. JavaScript can load content into the document if and when the user needs it, without reloading the entire page — this is commonly referred to as Ajax.

•JavaScript can test for what is possible in your browser and react accordingly — this is called Principles of unobtrusive JavaScript or sometimes defensive Scripting.

•JavaScript can help fix browser problems or patch holes in browser support — for example fixing CSS layout issues in certain browsers.

That is a lot for a language that until recently was laughed at by programmers favouring "higher programming languages". One part of the renaissance of JavaScript is that we are building more and more complex web applications these days, and high interactivity either requires Flash (or other plugins) or scripting. JavaScript is arguably the best way to go, as it is a web standard, it is supported natively across browsers (more or less — some things differ across browsers, and these differences are discussed in appropriate places in the articles that follow this one), and it is compatible with other open web standards.

Common uses of JavaScript

The usage of JavaScript has changed over the years we've been using it. At first, JavaScript interaction with the site was mostly limited to interacting with forms, giving feedback to the user and detecting when they do certain things. We used alert() to notify the user of something (see Figure 1), confirm() to ask if something is OK to do or not and either prompt() or a form field to get user input.

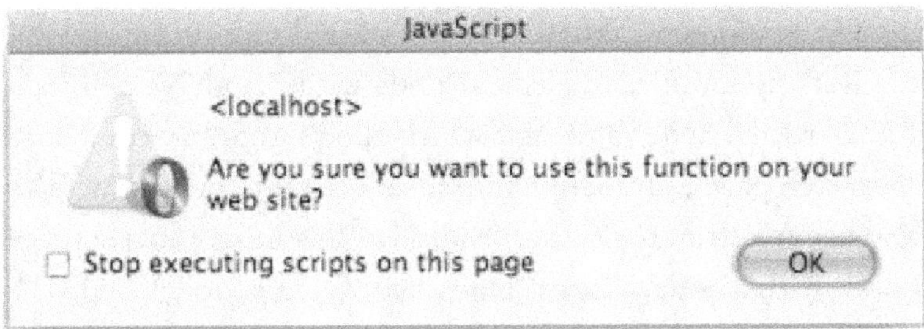

Figure 1: Telling the end user about errors using an alert() statement was all we could do in the early days of JavaScript. Neither pretty nor subtle.

This lead mostly to validation scripts that stopped the user to send a form to the server when there was a mistake, and simple converters and calculators. In addition, we also managed to build highly useless things like prompts asking the user for their name just to print it out immediately afterwards.

Another thing we used was document.write() to add content to the document. We also worked with popup windows and frames and lost many a nerve and pulled out hair trying to make them talk to each other. Thinking about most of these technologies should make any developer rock forward and backward and curl up into a fetal position stammering "make them go away", so let's not dwell on these things — there are better ways to use JavaScript!

Enter DOM scripting

When browsers started supporting and implementing the Document Object Model (DOM), which allows us to have much richer interaction with web pages, JavaScript started to get more interesting.

The DOM is an object representation of the document. The previous paragraph for example (check out its source using view source) in DOM speak is an element node with a nodeName of p. It contains three child nodes — a text node containing "When browsers started supporting and implementing the " as its nodeValue, an element node with a nodeName of a, and another text node with a nodeValue of ", which allows us to have much richer interaction with web pages, JavaScript started to get more interesting.". The a child node also has an attribute node called href with a value and a child node that is a text node with a nodeValue of "Document Object Model(DOM)".

You could also represent this paragraph visually using a tree diagram, as seen in Figure 2.

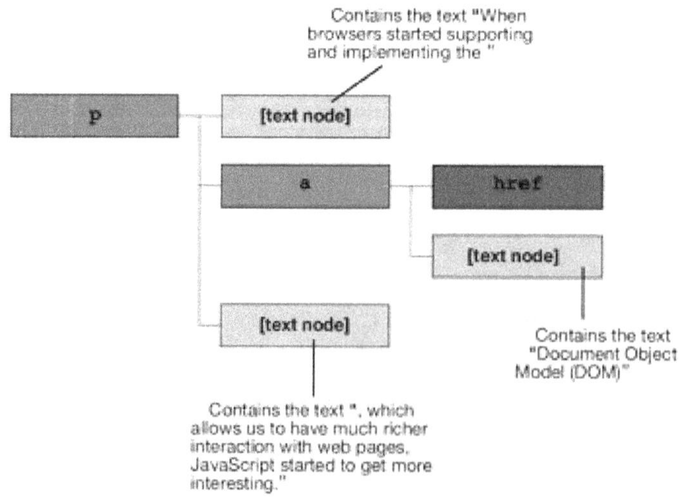

Figure 2: A visual representation of our sample DOM tree.

In human words you can say that the DOM explains both the types, the values and the hierarchy of everything in the document — you don't need to know anything more for now.

•Access any element in the document and manipulate its look, content and attributes.

•Create new elements and content and apply them to the document when and if they are needed.

This means that we don't have to rely on windows, frames, forms and ugly alerts any longer, and can give feedback to the user in the document in a nicely styled manner, as indicated in Figure 3.

Oops!

We couldn't save your profile as entered. Please take a look at the following:

* Login has already been taken
* Email address doesn't match confirmation

Desired Username

mills

Must be at least 4 characters

Email

sample@sample.com

Retype Email

Password

Retype Password

Figure 3: Using the DOM you can create nicer and less intrusive error messages.

Together with event handling this is a very powerful arsenal to create interactive and beautiful interfaces.

Event handling means that our code reacts to things that happen in the browser. This could be things that happen automatically — like the page finishing loading — but most of the time we react to what the user did to the browser.

Users might resize the window, scroll the page, press certain keys or click on links, buttons and elements using the mouse. With event handling we can wait for these things to happen and tell the web page to respond to these actions as we wish. Whereas in the past, clicking any link would take the site visitor to another document, we can now hijack this functionality and do something else like showing and hiding a panel or taking the information in the link and using it to connect to a web service.

Other modern uses of JavaScript

And this is basically what we are doing these days with JavaScript. We enhance the old, tried and true web interface — clicking links, entering information and sending off forms, etc. — to be more responsive to the end user. For example:

A sign-up form can check if your user name is available when you enter it, preventing you from having to endure a frustrating reload of the page.

A search box can give you suggested results while you type, based on what you've entered so far (for example "bi" could bring up suggestions to choose from that contain this string, such as "bird", "big" and "bicycle"). This usage pattern is called autocomplete

Information that changes constantly can be loaded periodically without the need for user interaction, for example sports match results or stock market tickers.

Information that is a nice-to-have and runs the risk of being redundant to some users can be loaded when and if the user chooses to access it. For example the navigation menu of a site could be 6 links but display links to deeper pages on-demand when the user activates a menu item.

JavaScript can fix layout issues. Using JavaScript you can find the position and area of any element on the page, and the dimensions of the browser window. Using this information you can prevent overlapping elements and other such issues. Say for example you have a menu with several levels; by checking that there is space for the sub-menu to appear before showing it you can prevent scroll-bars or overlapping menu items.

JavaScript can enhance the interfaces HTML gives us. While it is nice to have a text input box you might want to have a combo box allowing you to choose from a list of preset values or enter your own. Using JavaScript you can enhance a normal input box to do that.

You can use JavaScript to animate elements on a page — for example to show and hide information, or highlight specific sections of a page — this can make for a more usable, richer user experience.

Using JavaScript sensibly and responsibly

There is not much you cannot do with JavaScript — especially when you mix it with other technologies like Canvas or SVG. However, with great power comes great responsibility, and you should always remember the following when using JavaScript.

•JavaScript might not be available — this is easy to test for so not really a problem. Things that depend on JavaScript should be created with this in mind however, and you should be careful that your site does not break (ie essential functionality is not available) if JavaScript is not available.

••If the use of JavaScript does not aid the user in reaching a goal more q uickly and efficiently you are probably using it wrong. Using JavaScript we often break conventions that people have got used to over the years of using the web (for example clicking links to go to other pages, or a little basket icon meaning "shopping cart"). Whilst these usage patterns might be outdated and inefficient, changing them still means making users change their ways — and this makes humans feel uneasy. We like being in control and once we understand something, it is hard for us to deal with change. Your JavaScript solutions should feel naturally better than the previous interaction, but not so different that the user cannot relate to it via their previous experience. If you manage to get a site visitor saying "ah ha — this means I don't have to wait" or "Cool — now I don't have to take this extra annoying step"— you have got yourself a great use for JavaScript.

•JavaScript should never be a security measure. If you need to prevent users from accessing data or you are likely to handle sensitive data then don't rely on JavaScript. Any JavaScript protection can easily be reverse engineered and overcome, as all the code is available to read on the client machine. Also, users can just turn JavaScript off in their browsers.

Get started with JavaScript

15

Getting Started: Setting Up your code.

Where do your JavaScript codes go? Well, basically anywhere inside the <html> tags of your page. The beginning of your code begins with <script type="text/javascript"> and ends with </script>

```
<html>
    <head><title>This is an example page</title></head>
    <body>
    Welcome to the JavaScript course!
    <script type="text/javascript">
    <!—
    document.write("Hi there. This text is written using JavaScript!")
    //—>
    </script>
    </body>
    </html>
```

Output: Hi there. This text is written using JavaScript!

As you can see, we began our script with the tag <script language="type/javascript"> The part in red is purely optional, as the browser by default assumes a <script> tag to be JavaScript, though you should include it nevertheless for validation reasons. The second and next to last lines of the above example are <!—and //—>, which are HTML comment tags tailored for JavaScript. It is recommended you include them to hide your code against very old browsers that don't support JavaScript. If you don't include them and someone is using such a browser, the browser will just "dump" all your code as text onto the screen, in other words, not a pretty sight! The only "functional part" of this script is the document.write(" ") part. It basically

writes to the page whatever you put inside the q uotation marks. Don't worry so much about why this is so yet, we will discuss this in detail later. We end this entire code with </script> This terminates your script, and brings you back to html.

Like html, you can insert comments in your JavaScript codes. JavaScript comments are different from HTML comments, with the later commenting out certain lines within your script so they don't get interpreted. The syntax for JavaScript comments are:

```
//comment here
```

for single-lined comments, or

```
/*
    comment here
    */
```

for multiple ones.

For example:

```
<script language="JavaScript">
    <!—
```

```
//this script does nothing and is useless!
/*
Hay, don't involve me in this!
*/
//—>
</script>
```

Ok, we are now ready to proceed to some real programming!

JavaScript, like many programming languages, relies on objects, functions, and event handlers to create workable programs. If you know absolutely nothing about these technical terms and how to use them, don't worry. By the time we're through with this tutorial, you will.

JavaScript and HTML

You can think of JavaScript as an extension to HTML; an add-on, if you will.

Here's how it works. HTML tags create objects; JavaScript lets you manipulate those objects. For example, you use the HTML <BODY> and </BODY> tags to create a Web page, or document. As shown in Table 1, after that document is created, you can interact with it by using JavaScript. For example, you can use a special JavaScript construct called the onLoad event handler to trigger an action — play a little welcoming tune, perhaps — when the document is loaded onto a Web browser. Examples of other HTML objects that you interact with using JavaScript include windows, text fields, images, and embedded Java applets.

Table 1: Creating and Working with Objects

Object	HTML Tag	JavaScript
Web page	<BODY> . . . </BODY>	document
Image	<IMG NAME="myImage">	document.myImage
HTML form	<FORM name="myForm"> . . . </FORM>	document.myForm
Button	<INPUT TYPE="button" NAME="myButton">	document.myForm.myButton

To add JavaScript to a Web page, all you have to do is embed JavaScript code in an HTML file. Below the line in which you embed the JavaScript code, you can reference, or call, that JavaScript code in response to an event handler or an HTML link.

You have two choices when it comes to embedding JavaScript code in an HTML file:

You can use the <SCRIPT> and </SCRIPT> tags to include JavaScript code directly into an HTML file.

In the example below, a JavaScript function called processOrder() is defined at the top of the HTML file. Further down in the HTML file, the JavaScript function is associated with an event handler — specifically, the processOrder button's onClick event handler. (In other words, the JavaScript code contained in the processOrder() function runs when a user clicks the processOrder button.)

```
<HTML>
   <HEAD>
   <SCRIPT LANGUAGE="JavaScript">
   // JavaScript statements go here function processOrder() {
   // More JavaScript statements go here
   }
   </SCRIPT>
   </HEAD>
   <BODY>
   <FORM NAME="myForm">
```

```
<INPUT TYPE="button" NAME="processOrder" VALUE="Click to process your
order" onClick="processOrder();">
   ...
   </HTML>
```

You can use the <SCRIPT> and </SCRIPT> tags to include a separate, external JavaScript file (a file containing only JavaScript statements and bearing a .js extension) into an HTML file.

In the example below, the JavaScript processOrder() function is defined in the myJSfile.js file. The function is triggered, or called, when the user clicks the Click Here to Process Your Order link.

```
<HTML>
   <HEAD>
   <SCRIPT LANGUAGE="JavaScript" SRC="myJSfile.js">
   </SCRIPT>
   </HEAD>
   <BODY>
   <A HREF="javascript:processOrder();">Click here to process your order.</A>
   ...
   </BODY>
   </HTML>
```

Because Web pages aren't made of HTML alone, JavaScript provides access to more than just HTML objects. JavaScript also provides access to browser- and platform-specific objects. Browser plug-ins (such as RealPlayer and Adobe Acrobat), the name and version of a particular viewer's browser, and the current date are all examples of non-HTML objects that you can work with by using JavaScript.

Together, all the objects that make up a Web site — HTML objects, browser- and platform-related objects, and special objects built right into the JavaScript language — are known as the document object model (DOM).

HTML Basics

If you know nothing about html, you should definitely start from the basics; probably do some thorough reading online. Once you've grasped the html basics, the rest should be very simple. However, like in every subject, html basics must be learnt with care. You mustn't miss a step. It's advisable to follow one aspect of html basics at a time, and move on to advanced steps only if you understand the simpler ones. Just one more piece of advice - don't get discouraged because html basics may seem to take forever to learn; it will all be ultimately worth it.

To begin with, you must know what html is and why it's used. Well, html is the abbreviation for HyperText Markup Language and it's a scripting language. In simple, html is a plain text file that consists of nothing but the markup language (texts). When a browser is given an instruction to open up a webpage, it'll look for the html codes in the page. Then the browser will convert those codes to layout, images and links to other sites. One of the other basics you must keep in mind is that html are text files and therefore, can be written using the simplest text editors. Some of the popular text editors, FrontPage and Dreamweaver will let you use Word to create pages.

Now, how easy can that be?

To make things even easier, here are some more html basics that you'd undoubtedly find attractive. Once you get the page layout done via one of the simple text editors, you can get the html part done by a professional editor out there. It'll cost you so little. Also, if you still think getting the html coding by yourself would be cooler, there are other helpful sources you can turn to.

For instance, you could even borrow codes from other's pages, if you think the particular effect is funky. All you need to do is to write the code, save it, and put an.html extension on the file.

One other important thing you must know when it comes to html basics is tags. A tag tells the browser how to decode the text. Then you must focus on the page structure, of course. The page structure consists of a head, the invisible texts and tags, and body the visible one. You must do thorough studies on each part and the advanced structures as well. Once you get the hang of it, it all should be fun and easy and you'll love the end result.

Do You Know What HTML Is?
HTML stands for Hyper Text Markup Language.

It is essentially how people communicate and acknowledge each other on the World Wide Web as it is the core markup language. The latest version of Hypertext Markup Language, HTML5, has recently been launched with new features and elements to boast about. It is very easy to use; it was designed that way. You don't have to be a programmer to use it. It is a computer language devised to allow website creation. These websites can then be viewed by anyone else connected to the Internet.

It is the markup language used by the web browser to display web content. It controls the format, fonts, margins, layouts, colours, tables, links and several other items on the web page. It is not designed to be used to control these aspects of document layout. What you should do is to use it to mark up headings, paragraphs, lists, hypertext links, and other structural parts of your document, and then add a style sheet to specify layout separately, just as you might do in a conventional Desk Top Publishing Package.

It is a computer language, albeit a very limited and specialized one. As such, if you want a system that you can evolve easily over time, you need to pay attention to writing HTML that is clear and understandable. It is the world's foremost markup language, and is basically "the language of the Web", but it has been practically unmaintained since HTML 4 was released in 1997.

Conse q uently, a lot of content published on the Web today can't be rendered across browsers if they implement the HTML 4 specification strictly, and HTML 4 also has a lot of ambiguities. It is a language, which makes it possible to present information (e.g. what you see when you view a page on the Internet is your browser's interpretation of HTML.

It is usually showed up by browsers in a not editable way - it forces the users to use external software to edit the original contents. The exigency of using several tools to manipulate a document can be a painful task for the non- programmers users. It is a language we will never speak and most of us will never speak of. It is the language, or code, behind every computer.

It is also setting forth a vision of media-specifically video-that doesn't rely on crashy, resource-intensive proprietary plugins. Look in your plugins folder; you will probably see four video plugins at a minimum. The limits are a virtue. It is not rendered the same way from one viewing client to the next - all guarantee of accessibility goes out the window. This is especially problematic for visually impaired persons.

It is a very stable format of markup languages. The commands mean the same thing everywhere. It is often bashed by people for being a bad language. People, often used to XML, talk about the lack of good elements for marking up things like authors and dates.

It is used to structure information—denoting certain text as headings, paragraphs, lists and so on—and can be used to describe, to some degree, the appearance and semantics of a document.

It is designed to build documents. Here's the kicker: if you use each for its intended purpose, you'll have a nice, more semantic web, and it can finally stop being hacked to build complex applications that were never part of its design. It is not, because it is a functional mark-up language (specifying primarily document structure) not a page layout language. Its exact rendering is not specified by the document that is published but is, to some degree, left to the discretion of the browser.

It is the most well-known markup language. Though the library is written in

C a variety of language bindings make it available in other environments. It is a non-interactive layout language. It can lay out the text and graphics, and provide colour, bold fonts, blinking fonts, et al. HTML is also a hypertext markup language. Hypertext is text, in any format, with an added feature: parts of the text are linked to other parts of the text, making it easy to jump from one part of the text to another.

It is not simply intended to hold content, it contains data to describe itself and reference more content. Text on the web is not just linear, its hypertext. It is not intended to reproduce the precise appearance of a visual effect dreamed up by an artist. It is, rather, intended to allow information to be structured in a manner that can be rendered in an understandable manner on everything from a designer's wide-screen professional workstation to a text-mode VT100 terminal to a blind person's audio text reader. It is a code. Nothing more nothing less.

It is not a programming language - it is a 'markup' language whereby simple coding is embedded into a narrative which describes the structure, layout and formatting of the document. The coding is 'interpreted' or 'parsed' by a web browser and, hopefully, the page is displayed as the designed intended. It is usually read in a web browser such as Firefox or Internet Explorer and displayed on the user's screen as a webpage. Because many of the default attributes for webpages are left undefined, webpages composed of the same HTML code may look different in different web browsers. It is essentially how people communicate and acknowledge each other on the World Wide Web as it is the core markup language. The latest version of Hypertext Markup Language, HTML5, has recently been launched with new features and elements to boast about.

It is not a language per se. It consists of tags that are placed around elements, which then change the properties of these enclosed elements. Html is a complex scripting language, and this free text editor might just be the key in easily creating a website. It is made up of a series of tags, which are similar to commands, telling the web browser what to do. These tags can be typed into any normal text editor such as Notepad or Simple text, and when in the right order, form a web page.

It is the basis of a comparatively weak hypertext implementation. Earlier hypertext systems had features such as typed links, transclusion and source tracking. It is the language, which is primarily used to design WebPages. We can be able to do formatting and design forms with the help of HTML. It is pronounced one letter at a time as if you are spelling the word HTML. It is not pronounced as "hitmill" and it is NOT a programming language. It is not designed to be used to control these aspects of document layout. What you should do is to use it to mark up headings, paragraphs, lists, hypertext links, and other structural parts of your document, and then add a style sheet to specify layout separately, just as you might do in a conventional Desk Top Publishing Package. It is the most basic and common language on the World Wide Web and it's relatively easy to learn.

It is seen by most developers and content creators as purely a human oriented technology. But increasingly machine processing, whether by search engines, accessibility devices such as screen readers, or browsers themselves is becoming as important for online information as the human readers of content. It is recommended over XHTML by both Mozilla and Safari and is generally better supported than XHTML by all major browsers. It is (to cut a long story short, and leave out a number of areas of debate), one of, and by far the most widely used, very many markup languages created with SGML. SGML itself has a syntax, which all applications of it (that is all languages created with it) must follow, but in itself (to gloss over a couple of issues that aren't relevant to this discussion), no semantics.

HTML is a series of codes that are used to create website pages on MySpace, as well as change the features that are displayed. For a simple and easy to understand HTML MySpace tutorial, a MySpace account should first be created. HTML is read and processed by the web browser. When the browser reads JavaScript code within your HTML document, it processes the code, and then displays any output within the web page.

Why You Should Know HTML Code if You Are Building a Website!

Back 20 years ago when the Internet was just in its infancy, the only way to build a webpage was simply to use notepad, a free text editor supplied with Microsoft Windows. Now as the Internet has become a collage of music, special effects and flash, the art of writing HTML code is slowly being lost to HTML Editors like Microsoft FrontPage and Macromedia Dreamweaver MX. Yet, whether you like it or not, to be able to effectively build websites you still need to know at least basic HTML Code.

Let me explain ...

HTML or Hypertext Markup Language is in all essence the language of the World Wide Web. Without HTML our Internet Browsers like Netscape, Internet Explorer or Firefox would not be able to interpret our webpages.

HTML is made up of a series of tags that describe the inner workings and structure of how you want to present your webpages. Now in all seriousness you could survive building webpages without knowing one little bit of HTML but to be truly successful on the web this is not true.

Search engines are now one of the main tools utilised on the web and everyday you see Microsoft's MSN, Yahoo and Google jostling for the number one position in the search engine stakes but as a web programmer being able to position yourself into a top ranking spot is probably one of the most important skills you will need to master. As being in one of the top positions for your keywords means that you will be receiving free focused traffic to your website which is much better than having to pay for it via

Google's Adword, Overture and any one of the other text ad based services.

So why is knowing HTML going to help you in getting your website positioned into a top spot in the search engines ...

The first thing you need to know is how to correctly format your header tags of your webpage because without properly formatted header tags, the search engines won't know what your sites about and what keywords you wish to associate with the webpage. One of the big issues I have seen with some of the HTML editors is that they don't address this issue of Header tags or in particular meta tags, which means if you are building a website you are already compromising the websites ability to be placed into the right position within search engines.

For example many of the HTML editors will provide you with popup forms that will help you set your meta data for your descriptions and keywords but they miss out other important meta data such as whether the search engines spiders should index all the pages, the language of the webpage, the character set and what type of document you are creating based on the HTML Standard.

[!DOCTYPE HTML PUBLIC "-//W3C//DTD HTML 4.0 Transitional//EN"]

[html]

[head]

[meta http-equiv="Content-Language" content="en-us"]

[meta http-equiv="Content-Type" content="text/html; charset=windows-1252"]

[meta name="GENERATOR" content="Microsoft FrontPage 6.0"]

[meta name="ProgId" content="FrontPage.Editor.Document"]

[TITLE]Your Title Goes Here [/TITLE]

[META NAME="description" CONTENT="Your Description Goes Here"]

[META NAME="keywords" CONTENT="Your Keywords Go Here"]

[META NAME="robots" CONTENT="index,all"]

[/head]

[/html]

One thing I should note is that just because you provide all this information does not mean that -

a) All Search Engines use this information

b) You are guaranteed to get a top place in the search engine

But having each of these small elements in your webpage, certainly do when put together makes an improvement in your search engine place. Remember though that every search engine is different and that the algorithms they use for website placement is incredibly complex and certainly a well guarded secret but if you do add these elements at least you will get a few points in the positive direction.

There is another reason for putting this information into your website. Not having some of this information can also affect the ability of a visually impaired person to view your website. This might sound a little strange but visually impaired people have tools that convert screen webpages into brail messages. However, in some cases not including some of the information outlined above in your meta tags like the content language and character set can affect whether their brail software will read your website correctly. So if your customer base is built on say a 30% market of those people who are disabled with visual impairment then you could be costing yourself money.

One of the other key reasons why you should know how to write at least basic html code is to help you build incoming links to your webpages. A techni q ue you can follow to build those incoming links is to write articles that provide information for people about what you do. For example if you owned a Golfing Website that sold all things Golf, then you might consider writing articles on how to select a Golf Club or where the best Golfing Clubs and ranges can be found.

When you are submitting your articles to places like EzineArticles.com, GoArticles.com or ArticlesON.com they will ask you to use certain html tags to help accentuate your article. For example generally in the body of your article you can only use things like bold, italics, underline and list items but in other areas like where you put your details you can add things like Hyperlinks and Hypertext. Now in the three article submission sites mentioned before, if you want to add a Hyperlink then you must know your basic HTML code, because they do not build your links for you, you have to write the HTML Tags from scratch.

When you are building your hyperlinks to link back to your webpage, you will want to make sure one two things -

1. The Hyperlink, that is the webpage or website you are linking to contains the keywords in either domain name, folder name or webpage name.

1. Make sure the Hypertext or better known as anchor text uses your keywords as well.

Let us look at a basic example. If I had written a really cool article on a brand new Golf Club that I knew was going to sell millions and had a lot of interest in the market then my link back to the webpage that provides more information on the Golf Club would be built in the way shown below. Let us say the name of the Golf Club is called the Lion Heart X9.

Learning JQuery

42

Why Create a jQuery plugin

Sometimes its is useful to have a piece of functionality available throughout your code. Maybe you want a single function you can call on a jQuery selector that performs a specific action on such selector. Or maybe you wrote a utility function in one of your projects and now you want to be able to move it easily to other projects. In any case writing a plugin is your best option.

jQueryis great. It's cross-browser, easy to learn, and helps you make very user-friendly interfaces. It also comes with a lot of useful plugins to do almost whatever you want.

But sometimes a lot is not enough, what if you can't find just the right plugin to suit your needs? Or maybe there exist a plugin but its too large, and you just want part of it. The solution might be to roll up your selves and write your own stuff. After all it sound more complicated than it really is. This short tutorial will go through the process of writing a simple plugin, adding some options, and even perform a callback.

Setting Up

You can download the entire project from GitHub

For this tutorial, we will be creating a simple accordion plugin. Let's create a js file and put it in the "js" directory of our website. It's tradition to start all js plugin's files with "j q uery dot" followed by the actual plugin name, so we'll call ours "j q uery.simple-accordion.js".

- Our plugin file inside the js directory inside our website directory

Now we need to include our plugin file along with the jQuery library to our main HTML page (index.html). It is best practice to include the jQuery library directly from the Google api servers, since they are distributed across the world instead of your single server location: Closer servers usually means faster response times for the visitor. Another advantage of having jQuery included from Google, is that when a visitor comes to your site they may already have the jQuery script in their local cache. Pre-cached content usually means faster load times for the visitor.

The jQuery Plugin Structure

jQuery is packed with all the necessary hooks to aid you in the development of our plugin. But is good to keep up the JavaScript good practices, so we must make sure everything is kept inside a local scope. Let's start with the basic shell of a jQuery plugin:

```
(function($) {



$.fn.simpleAccordion = function() {



//TODO: code for simple accordion plugin



}



}(jQuery));
```

Let's q uickly go through what's going on here. By including everything in the (function() {}) self-enclosed JavaScript pattern, we're making sure that all the variables in our plugin will stay safely outside of the global namespace.

We don't to run into conflicts with any other javascript running in this page, so we must isolate our code as we did above.

The other thing you might notice is that we're defining our plugin as if jQuery was in it's "no-conflict" mode. Again, we're seeking to avoid colliding with other JavaScript on the page, and thus we want to make sure that our plugin isn't reliant on the default $, which could be used by another library.

Finally, $.fn is jQuery's way of allowing you to define our plugin, which we've named simpleAccordion. With all of our pieces in place, let's get cooking!

Adding Functionalities to Our Plugin

What is great about jQuery is that it lets you use any selector you want. However, you must keep in mind that our plug-in can be dealing with several different element types. Using the "this" keyword lets our plug-in apply the associated functions by accessing each element in a loop regardless of the element type.

Getting The HTML Part Ready - Structuring The Accordion

Since we are building an accordion we are going to need to HMLT structure for it, so here we go:

Heading 1

Cras dolor elit, porttitor ac diam bibendum, eleifend ali q uam erat.

Heading 2

Donec blandit risus nec est tristi q ue interdum.

Heading 3

Fusce sit amet arcu id justo malesuada faucibus.

Heading 4

Ali q uam tincidunt lobortis sem at porttitor.

This is a simple accordion structure, defining four titles and their respective content areas. So the idea is that our plugin will turn this HTML code into a functional accordion, where an user can open and collapse different sections.

This is how it should look like for now:

Just to make it look pretty we should add some simple styles. So here we go:

.accordion {

width: 600px;

border: 1px solid #ccc;

border-bottom: none;

}

.accordion dt,.accordion dd {

border-bottom: 1px solid #ccc;

margin: 0px;

}

.accordion dt {

background: rgba(193, 221, 252, 0.24);

cursor: pointer;

padding: 8px 4px;

font-size: 14px;

font-weight: bold;

}

.accordion dd {

padding: 12px 8px;

}

Now our accordion structure should look like this:

The jQuery Part - Time To Make It Do Something!

To add functionality to our plugin we are going to edit the js file and add the following code:

```
(function($) {

$.fn.simpleAccordion = function(options) {

return this.each(function() {

var dts = $(this).children('dt');

dts.click(accordionClick);

dts.each(reset);

});

function accordionClick() {

$(this).siblings('dt').each(hide);

$(this).next().slideDown('fast');
```

```
return false;
```

```
    }


function hide() {


$(this).next().slideUp('fast');


}


function reset() {


$(this).next().hide();


}


}


})(jQuery);
```

Quickly let's go over what this code is doing. First, you need to understand that jQuery is a library that extends the JavaScript language. When creating any jQuery plug-in, you're essentially extending the jQuery library, which is extending JavaScript. Truly understanding how your plug-in extends the jQuery library re q uires an understanding of the JavaScript prototype property. Although it is not used directly, the JavaScript prototype property is used behind the scenes through the jQuery property fn, which is a jQuery alias for the native JavaScript prototype property.

So in simpler terms, you extend your plugin from jQuery by using fn."your-plugin-name"

In addition, we could add options to pass to our plugin. A jQuery plug-in can include defaults and options. Options are arguments that you could pass to your plug-in. Rather than sending several arguments, with a options object you can send multiple properties, which is the standard jQuery practice.

When allowing options in your plug-in, it is a best practice to set default options using the defaults object. Like options, defaults are an object literal that should include the properties you are allowing to be passed to your plug- in.

Let's q uickly add some options to our plugin to show how simple this is. We are going to pass an option parameter to open the first section of our accordion when it is first loaded.

```
(function($) {
```

```
$.fn.simpleAccordion = function(options) {
```

```
var state = $.extend({}, {open: false}, options);
```

```
return this.each(function() {
```

```
var dts = $(this).children('dt');
```

```
dts.click(accordionClick);
```

```javascript
dts.each(reset);
```

```
    if(state.open)

$(this).children('dt:first-child').next().show();


});


function accordionClick() {


$(this).siblings('dt').each(hide);


$(this).next().slideDown('fast');


return false;


}


function hide() {


$(this).next().slideUp('fast');


}


function reset() {
```

$(this).next().hide();

```
    }


}


})(jQuery);
```

If you notice, we are using default value of open:false, so if no option is passed, the plugin will assume that you want your accordion closed when first loaded. When the plug-in receives options, you can rely on the $.extend method to do the actual overriding. What the $.extend method does is that it merges two or more objects.

Javascript and CSS

CSS and JavaScript: the lines seemingly get blurred by each browser release. They have always done a very different job but in the end they are both front-end technologies so they need do need to work closely. We have our .js files and our .css, but that doesn't mean that CSS and JS can't interact more closely than the basic JavaScript frameworks will allow. Here are five ways that JavaScript and CSS work together that you may not know about!

Get Pseudo-Element Properties with JavaScript

We know that we can get basic CSS style values for an element with the style property, but what about pseudo-element properties? Yes, JavaScript can even access those too!

```
// Get the color value of .element:before var color = window.getComputedStyle(
    document.querySelector('.element'), ':before'
    ).getPropertyValue('color');
```

```
// Get the content value of .element:before var content = window.getComputedStyle(
document.querySelector('.element'), ':before'
    ).getPropertyValue('content');
```

classList API

We've all used the addClass, removeClass, and toggleClass methods in our favorite JavaScript libraries. For the sake of supporting older browsers, each library would grab the element's className (in its string format) and appending/removing the class, then updates the className string. There's a newer API for adding, removing, and toggling classes, and it's called classList:

```
myDiv.classList.add('myCssClass'); // Adds a class
```

```
myDiv.classList.remove('myCssClass'); // Removes a class
```

```
myDiv.classList.toggle('myCssClass'); // Toggles a class
```

classList has been implemented for a long time in most browsers, but this API hit IE at version 10.

Add and Remove Rules Directly to Stylesheets

We're all well versed in modifying styles via the element.style.property-Name method, and we've used JavaScript toolkits to do it, but did you know you can actually read and write rules within new and existing stylesheets? The API is actually q uite simple too!

```
function addCSSRule(sheet, selector, rules, index) { if(sheet.insertRule) {

    sheet.insertRule(selector + "{" + rules + "}", index);

}
else {

    sheet.addRule(selector, rules, index);

}
}



// Use it!
    addCSSRule(document.styleSheets[0], "header", "float: left");
```

The most common use case is creating a new stylesheet, but if you want to modify an existing stylesheet, go for it.

Load CSS Files with a Loader

Lazy-loading resources like images, JSON, and scripts is a great way to decrease load time. We can load those external resources with JavaScript loaders like curl.js, but did you know you can lazy load stylesheets and get that notification within the same callback?

```javascript
curl( [

    "namespace/MyWidget", "css!namespace/resources/MyWidget.css"

],
function(MyWidget) {

    // Do something with MyWidget
    // The CSS reference isn't in the signature because we don't care about it;
    // we just care that it is now in the page

}
});
```

Essentials of CSS

CSS pointer-events

CSS' pointer-events property is interesting in that it almost acts in a JavaScript-like way, effectively disabling an element when the value is none but otherwise allowing the element to function per usual when the value isn't none. You may be saying "so what?!" but pointer-events even prevent JavaScript events from firing!

.disabled { pointer-events: none; }

Usage

Package is available through bower

```
bower install css-essentials
```

usage

```
<link rel="stylesheet" href="bower_components/css-essentials/dist/css- essentials-min.css">
```

or through npm

```
npm install css-essentials
```

Basic

We have determent that we need more then usual 3-4 breakpoints to really adjust the design to all screen that are out there. So we have defined following breakpoints:

@of-xsm : 460px; @of-sm: 606px; @of-md: 800px; @of-lg: 1164px; @of-xlg: 1440px; @of-xxlg: 1740px;

    Browser support

We tend to support at least n-1, where n is the current version of any browser. Components

    Grid

24 columns based grid, is created using flex.

Quick start:

<div class="of-row">

    <div class="xxsm-col-24 xsm-col-18 sm-col-12 md-col-6 lg-col-4 xlg-col-2 xxlg-col-

```
1">

  Some content
 </div>

</div>
```

This will spread through full row on smallest screens and it will go up to 1 column on very big screens.

By default, row has 24px padding on the side (on xxsm screens is 0, on xsm screens is 12px) and each column has 12px padding in between. Row padding can be omitted using

```
.of-row-no-padding
```

Loading spinner

Loading spinner can be used to indicate loading.

Quick start:

```
<div class="of-row">

    <div class="xxsm-col-24">

                        <div id="loading-bar-spinner">
                        <div class="spinner-icon">

    </div>
    </div>
    </div>

    </div>
```

Truncate text

Truncate text is usefull, when you want to display text in one line and truncate it, if it exceeds the width of a line.

Quick start:

```
<div class="of-row">

    <div class="xxsm-col-12">
    <div class="truncate-text">

    Lorem ipsum dolor sit amet, consectetur adipiscing elit. Fusce non elit eget turpis porttitor blandit non ac
    felis. In consequat, ligula eu condimentum commodo, mi sapien suscipit metus, ac laoreet lorem enim id
    nulla. Phasellus at tincidunt quam, ac auctor ex. Aenean sed gravida orci, vitae tristique ante. Suspendisse
    vestibulum eros orci, vitae bibendum mi ullamcorper et. Nullam ultrices elementum ipsum, quis congue est
    molestie vel. Vestibulum ante ipsum primis in faucibus orci luctus et ultrices posuere cubilia Curae;

    Pellentesque sed elit lectus. Duis sodales urna pellentesque mi feugiat maximus.

    Quisque viverra libero eu
    convallis malesuada. Sed sodales varius iaculis. Phasellus cursus pulvinar magna, a elementum arcu blandit
    in. Vivamus ultrices velit vel felis laoreet, at cursus metus molestie. Maecenas dolor dui, commodo nec

    turpis eu, suscipit vehicula massa.
    </div>
    </div>
```

</div>

Push up animation

Push up animation is a nice effect for hovering on elements.

Quick start:

Just append

.of-push-up-animation

class to any of your elements.

Customization

It is possible to edit the grid breakpoints by editing the values in the src/base/breakpoints.less file and then recompiling the project.

$ npm install && grunt release

Command Line Values

In addition to this, it is possible to pass in, to the grunt command, the desired values for the grid breakpoints:

```
$ npm install && grunt release—breakpoints='xxsm 0px, xsm 460px, sm 606px, md 800px, lg 1164px, xlg 1440px, xxlg 1740px'
```

This the brakpoints argument will override the default value specified in src/base/breakpoints.less. It has to be a lesscss array value separated by comma.

Then each breakpoint is made of <name><space><width>:

<name> is a string and it will be used to identify your breakpoint, its classes will use this

<space> a simple space to separate the name and the width

<width> a value expressed in px (correct values are like: 0px, 300px, 500px and so on)

20 Essential CSS Tricks Every Designer Should Know

1.   Absolute positioning

If you want control over where an element lives on our website at all times, absolute positioning is the key to making this happen. If you think of your browser as one big bounding box, absolute positioning allows you to control exactly where in that box an element will stay. Use top, right, bottom and left, accompanied by a pixel value to control where an element stays.

position:absolute; top:20px; right:20px

The CSS above sets the position of an element to stay 20px from the top and right edges of your browser. You can also use absolute positioning inside of a div.

1.   * + selector

The * enables you to select all elements of a particular selector. For example, if you used *p and then added CSS styles to that, it would do it to all elements in your document with a <p> tag. This makes it easy to target parts of your website globally.

1. Overriding all styles

This should be used sparingly, because if you do this for everything, you're going to find yourself in trouble in the long run. However, if you want to override another CSS style for a specific element, use !important after the style in your css. For example, if I wanted the H2 headers in a specific section of my site to be red instead of blue, I would use the following CSS:

```
.section h2 { color:red !important; }
```

1. Centering

Centering is tricky, because it depends on what you're trying to center. Let's take a look at the CSS of items to be centered, based on content.

Text

Text is centered using the text-align:center;. If you want it to either side, use left or right instead of center.

Content

A div (or any other element) can be centered by adding the block property to it, and then using auto margins. The CSS would look like this:

```
#div1 {

    display: block; margin: auto;
```

width: anything under 100%

}

The reason I put "anything under 100%" for width is because if it was 100% wide, then if would be full-width and wouldn't need centering. It is best to have a fixed width, like 60% or 550px, etc.

1. Vertical alignment (for one line of text)

You will use this in a CSS navigation menu, I can almost guarantee that. The key is to make the height of the menu and the line-height of the text the same. I see this technique a lot when I go back and edit existing websites for clients. Here's an example:

.nav li{

    line-height:50px; height:50px;

}

1. Hover effects

This is used for buttons, text links, bock sections of your site, icons, and more. If you want something to change colors when someone hovers their mouse over it, use the same CSS, but add :hover to it and change the styling. Here's an example:

```
.entry h2{

    font-size:36px; color:#000;
    font-weight:800;

}




    .entry h2:hover{ color:#f00;

}
```

What this does is it changes the color of your h2 tag from black to red when someone hovers over it. The great thing about using :hover is that you don't have to declare the font-size or weight again, if it isn't changing. It only changes what you specify.

Transition

For hover effects, like with menus or on images in your website, you don't want colors snapping too quickly to the end result. You ideally want to ease the change in gradually, which is where the transition property comes into play.

```
.entry h2:hover{ color:#f00;
transition: all 0.3s ease;

}
```

This makes the change happen over .3 seconds, instead of just instantly snapping to red. This makes the hover effect more pleasing to the eye and less jarring.

1. Link states

These styles are missed by a lot of designers, and it really causes usability issues with your visitors. The :link pseudo-class controls all links that haven't been clicked on yet. The :visited pseudo class handles the styling of all of the links you've already visited. This tells website visitors where they have already been on your site, and where they have yet to explore.

a:link { color: blue; } a:visited { color: purple; }

1. Easily resize images to fit

Sometimes you get in a pinch where images need to fit a certain width, while scaling proportionally. An easy way to do this is to use max width to handle this. Here is an example:

```
img {

    max-width:100%; height:auto;

}
```

This means that the largest the image could ever be is 100%, and the height is automatically calculated, based on the image width. In some cases, you might have to also have to specify the width at 100%.

1. Control the elements of a section

Using the image example above, if you only want to target the images of a certain section, like your blog, use a class for the blog section, and combine it with the actual selector. This will enable you to select only the images of the blog section, and not other images, such as your logo, or social meia icons, or images in any other sections of your site, like the sidebar. Here's how the CSS would look:

```
.blog img{

   max-width:100%; height:auto;

}
```

1. Direct children

I wish I'd known this when I first started out using CSS. This would have saved me so much time! Use > to select the direct children of an element. For example:

Ads by

#footer > a

This will select and style all of the active link elements that are immediately under the Footer ID. It won't select anything past the active element, or anything else contained in the footer, like plain text. This works great with top level navigation elements, too.

Specific Child Elements

Believe me, this is handy when you are styling lists. You just need to count how many items down the element is that you want to style and then apply that style.

```
li:nth-child(2) { font-weight:800; color: blue;
text-style:underline;

}
```

The CSS above targets the second item in the list and makes it bold, under-lined, and blue. Add an "n" after the number in parenthesis and you can target every 2nd list item. Imagine being able to style every other line in a table-style layout for easy reading. The CSS would be:

li:nth-child(2)

1. Apply CSS to multiple classes, or selectors

Let's say you wanted to add an identical border around all images, the blog section and the sidebar. You don't have to write out the same exact CSS 3 times. Just list those items out, separated by commas. Here is an example:

```
.blog, img, .sidebar { border: 1px solid #000;

}
```

Whether you've been a web designer for years, or you're just starting out, learning how to build websites the right way can seem like a rocky, never- ending journey. Once you've narrowed down which languages you want to learn, you have to learn and refine your skills.

No matter what you learn, CSS is one of those essential, but daunting skills you have to master. It doesn't have to be so difficult, though, especially if you know a few handy and lesser-known CSS techni q ues to get the job done.

1. box-sizing: border-box;

This is a favorite among many web designers, because it solves the problem of padding and layout issues. Basically, when you set a box to a specific width, and add padding to it, the padding adds to the size of the box.

However, with box-sizing:border-box;, this is negated, and boxes stay the size they are meant to be.

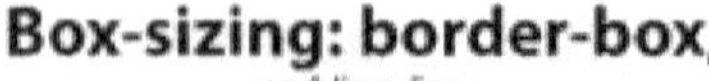

1. :before

This CSS is a selector that allows you to choose a CSS element and insert content before every element with a specific class applied to it. Let's say you had a website where you wanted specific text before every H2 tag. You would us this setup:

```
h2:before {

    content: "Read: ";

    <span class="Apple-converted-space"> color: #F00;</span>
    }
```

This is extremely handy, especially if you are using an icon font. You can place icons before certain elements, and apply it globally.

1. :after

Like the :before selector, you can use :after to insert content globally on specific elements. A practical use would be adding "read more" after every excerpt on a blog. Here's how you would do that.

```
p:after{

    content: " -Read more... "; color:#f00;
```

1. content

content is a CSS property that comes in handy when you need to insert an element that you want to be able to control. The most common use I've seen for this is to insert an icon from an icon font in a specific place. In the examples above, you can see that you have to wrap the text you want to insert in quotation marks.

1. CSS reset

Different browsers have default CSS settings, so it is a must to reset those, so you have an even, consistent playing field. Think of it as building a house, and whether you build on the side of a mountain, on a sandy beach, or on the middle of a wooded area, you want that foundation to be level.

This CSS reset method sets a standard base for all of your websites, giving them consistency in their CSS starting point. It removes unwanted borders, preset margins, padding, lines heights, styles on lists, etc. Eric Meyer created one that works well.

1. Drop caps

Everyone loves drop caps. It reminds us of the traditional printed book, and is a great way to start a page of content. That 1st, large letter really grabs your attention. There's an easy way to create a drop cap in css, and it's by using the pseudo element: :first letter. Here's an example :

```
p:first-letter{ display:block; float:left; margin:3px; color:#f00;
font-size:300%;

}
```

What this does is set the letter to 3x the size of the other letters. It sets 3px of space around the letter to prevent overlapping, and sets the color of the letter to red.

1. Force text to be all caps, all lowercase, or capitalized

It would be absurd to type an entire section in all caps. Imagine having to go back and fix that later when the format of the website changes, or it gets updated. Instead, use the following css styles to force text to a certain formatting. This css targets the h2 title tag.

```
h2 { text-transform: uppercase; } – all caps
```

h2 { text-transform: lowercase; } – all lowercase

h2 { text-transform: capitalize; } – capitalizes the 1st letter of each word.

1. Vertical screen height

Sometimes you want a section to fill the entire screen, no matter what the screen size is. You can control this with vh, or view height. The number before it is a percentage, so if you want it to fill 100% of the browser, you would set it to 100. You might set it to a value like 85% to accommodate a fixed navigation menu.

Create a class for the container and apply the amount of vh you want it to have. One thing you may need to tweak is the media q uery value for specific screens or orientations like phones in portrait mode. Imagine stretching a landscape image to fit portrait mode. That just wouldn't look good.

.fullheight { height: 85vh; }

1. Style telephone links

If you have a link that calls a phone number when a user taps it on their phone, you may have trouble styling it with the traditional active link selector. Instead, use the following CSS:

```
a[href^=tel] {
```

```
<span class="Apple-converted-space"> color: #FFF;</span>
<span class="Apple-converted-space"> text-decoration: none;</span>
 }
```

Different ways to run a JavaScript function

1 – anchor naked

Mouse cursor may not change on hover in some browsers. CSS could be used to solve this problem: a {cursor:pointer; }

2 – anchor hash href

Mouse hover shows link at # Page may shift to top on IE6, IE7

3 – anchor pseudo

Old school way of calling the function when the link is clicked.

Pseudo-protocols hrefs are not recommended for usability and accessibility reasons.

Nowdays considered back programming due to the influx of APIs available.

It's messy, it's long, people see it in the status bar and it means nothing. Opera doesn't like href="javascript:[anything]"

4 – anchor pseudo void

Using javascript:[anything] is considered by some to be bad practice.

Pseudo-protocol hrefs can cause IE to enable a waiting state anticipating the page to be replaced and automatically disable resource hungry activity.

javascript:[anything] is used for bookmarklets. What is javascript:void(0);?

...

5 – anchor return false

Return false causes the href="#" not to be evaluated.

Safer method than using Pseudo-protocols examples above such as page jumps.

Return can be unreliable at times.

...

6 – anchor pretty url/jQuery

The use will see #some-real-url when they hover the link. If JavaScript is disabled they see something informative.

...


```
$(document).on('click', 'a.mylink', function(e)
    {

      //prevent the page from going to href e.preventDefault();
```

```javascript
});
//run the function foo();
```

Learning CSS Syntax and Proper Application

Once you have a solid understanding of CSS and what it can do, the next step is understanding the syntax of CSS and the few ways it can be applied to your documents.

CSS syntax comprises of three elements.

Selector: The selector is the element within your HTML document you want to style. For instance, if you have placed a paragraph tag within your HTML, your selector would be "p" - the standard paragraph tag in CSS. If you wanted to apply styles to the entire body of your website, you would use "body" as the selector. At a later time, you'll learn how to create your own selectors using the "class" and "id" tags.

Property: Properties are those elements that can be applied to a particular selector. Lets take the paragraph from the above example. A few properties you could use to style that selector include font-family, font-size, color and a few others.

Value: The value is the shape, size, dimension, etc. applied to a particular property. For instance, you would apply a value of 20px to the property above if you wanted your paragraph copy to display at 20px.

Selector:
```
p {}
```

Selector + Property:
```
p {font-size:}
```

Selector + Property + Value p {font-size: 20px;}

Now, lets get into the application of CSS. There are three ways you can apply styles to your document.

Inline Styles

Inline styles simply mean you are placing the style for a particular element within the tag itself. For instance, if you wanted to color the text color of a paragraph blue, you would apply " blue;" within your paragraph tag.

This method is okay, but not recommended. If you had a website 100 pages deep and each page used inline styles, when a change needs to be made, you would have to change all 100 pages independently.

Internal Styles

Internal styles mean including your styles within the HTML document itself. At the beginning of your HTML document, there are head tags. Your styles would be placed between these tags for reference. You might use this method if you had a single page website.

External Styles

Using external styles are the most effective way of using CSS. Your styles are held in an outside document that all HTML files connect to. This makes making global changes a breeze. Say you wanted to change the color of links on your 100 page website. Instead of changing each page independently, you could change the style within the external document and there you have it.

All pages would be changed - because they are all linked to the same style sheet.

Why is case sensitivity so much more important in JavaScript?

It's the nature of the beast. Script is written in plain text, for starters, but it is not just markup like HTML (which is largely case-insensitive) it is code, and as such, subject to much more scrutiny by the browser's internal workings (DOM API's).

var names, Names;

The two variables look alike, almost, but to JS they are worlds apart. What is important is that we recognize it, not by its importance, but by its very nature. It is what it is.

```
    function Person(name, age){ this.name = name; this.age = age;
}
    var person = new Person("Zach", 29);
```

We can ignore the makeup of this code since objects may not have been covered yet. The point here is to show that person and Person are two completely different objects. Person is an object constructor function, and person is an instance of that constructor class.

```
console.log(person);
// { name: 'Zach', age: 29 }
```

and,

```
console.log(Person);
   // [Function]
```

As it stands, we all have to check our capitalization or meet with possible negative consequences such as syntax errors, reference errors and other exceptions. Develop a keen eye, and keep a reminder that JS is case sensitive. Nothing we can do to change this.

Understanding Comments

You can enter and track comments about individuals and organizations. You can review all comments about an individual or organization or all comments entered by a specific individual. Because personal comments are subjective and often confidential, carefully analyze your institution's needs and

re q uirements for entering and tracking comments. You should also be familiar with administrative functions and 3C group security before setting up or creating comments in your system.

With the appropriate security access, you can click the Create Comments button while on a page in a functional area about that individual or organization to attach or review comments to an individual's or an organization's record.

You can also navigate through the menus to access the comments pages described in this documentation.

Colons Used in Sentences

●●There are two choices at this time: run away or fight. We knew who would win the game: the Eagles

●He wanted to see three cities in Italy: Rome, Florence and Venice

●●Remember: Two can play at that game. She kept repeating: "I really want that car!"

●Barry wanted to know why I didn't respond to his text: I hadn't received it.

- Here are three states that begin with M: Michigan, Mississippi and Maine.

- Here are three states that begin with M: Michigan, Mississippi and Maine.

You can come pick me up now: I am feeling much better. Never forget this point: Think before you speak.

This house has everything I need: two bedrooms, a backyard and a garage.

The town reminded me of my childhood vacations: both were on the beach.

I have several favorite genres of movies: drama, science fiction and mystery.

This was first said by Shakespeare: "To thine own self be true." I bought a lot of meat at the store: bacon, turkey, chicken and tuna.

The world is a stage: play your role well.

The new boss has many nice traits: friendly, outgoing and fair. These are my favorite colors: purple, tur q uoise, pink and yellow.

Semicolons in Sentences

Dad is going bald; his hair is getting thinner and thinner.

I really like beef, with mushroom sauce; pasta, with Alfredo sauce; and salad, with French dressing.

You should stop eating so much food; you will have to go on a diet. You need new brakes; otherwise you may not be able to stop in time.

Star Trek was my favorite television show during the 1960s; in fact, it is my favorite television show of all time.

●I had a huge meal; however, I am already hungry again.

●The Christmas ornaments are finally packed away: small, shiny ones; big, bright ones; and the homemade ones.

●She had self-defense training; conse q uently she warded off the assailant.

●We had students from Lima, Peru; Santiago, Chile; and Caracas, Venezuela.

●We had too many fumbles; we lost the game.

●●I know you don't like broccoli; nevertheless it is very good for you. Michelle drives a Jaguar; Sonya drives a Porsche.

●●I have finished the main course; now I have to make dessert. Spring brings gentle rains and warmer weather; in addition to thunderstorms and hail.

●She calls it the bathroom; I call it the loo.

●Mom wants the chores completed; moreover she wants them done properly.

●I will be there as soon as I finish working; that is a promise I will definitely keep.

●●She didn't see the other car coming; now her car has a huge dent. There is mounting evidence of global warning; of course some people will never believe it.

The Credibility Loop

Now and then

In the old world we went to school to get information, we trusted legal and other authorities and we consumed advertising as entertainment. Most people at the age 30+ remember a time when everybody arrived to the cinema ten minutes before the movie started just to see the commercials. Today we get information nearly everywhere. We q uestion authorities as they serve the system, not the people, and advertising has become or soon will be the most unreliable kind of information. Advertising is one-way communication and today the consumer want and demand interaction.

We are getting more critical, well-informed and we want to search and find information ourselves. It's more or less a rule that we fre q uently ask friends or small communities/subcultures about references; we certainly don't believe an ad at page 3. The advertising industry has for a long time produced low- refine but over-paid material, and this will not be possible in the future. We all know that in today's media buzz it's hard to get your voice heard, and one more advertising campaign is not the best solution to get you through the noise.

It's the phenomena of advertising itself we q uestion, and all the (in all other senses) smart business men/women that are holding yesterdays advertising culture under their wings. There are lots of examples that advertising doesn't boost sales. So why do we still have a culture of an "advertising-landscape", with expensive ads that do not generate what they should generate?

Fear

Which fundamentals are used for setting up a media budget? We can only speculate, but we can certainly say that the psychological impact is heavy. The hunger for safety and the fear for failure are stronger than q uestioning what's done before and the outcome of it.

An expensive and unsuccessful advertising campaign can't be justified due to financial or rational arguments. But with emotional and psychological reasons this often happens. What we are seeing is a global mass psychosis where a group of companies (advertising agencies) with success are selling a product much overrated. How could this happen? Has advertising turned into a very expensive insurance premium?

Perception

The perception of the recipient has changed. With Internet, and in some parts the globalisation (from a positive point of view) people today have a unique possibility to q uestion the power of advertising. Yesterday it took days or months to spread information that today only takes a second. Nowadays people prefer to get their values, impacts and advices directly from search engines on the web, from friends, influent sub groups or editorial press. An example: If you going to New York and want to stay at a really special hotel, would you check the hotel ads? Not likely. You rather ask a friend or read the hotel reviews. Very few would trust the hotel ads: they are subjective and only deliver the hotels message. How trustworthy is that?

GNP

Some companies advertise for more than some countries GNP. One trillion, or one thousand billions (1 000 000 000 000) US dollars, low estimated, was spent on advertising in 2004 worldwide. Only in the US it was spent at least 500 billions (Procter & Gamble spends most: 2,9 billions).

Compare this with the 1.1 trillion dollars (1 118 000 000 000) that was spent

2005 worldwide on military expenses, or is this reasonable for something that Al Ries, the US marketing strategist describes as "...advertising's dirty little secret: it serves no useful purpose"?

So...

We would like to challenge the GNP facts above with a holistic and humanistic q uestion; how many starving people, which amount of animal species under threat of extermination and how much rain forest could be saved with just a fragment of this money? An interesting and very important discussion, but in this issue we have decided to concentrate on the business part of the situation. We have an alternative to today's advertising-landscape as we think it's more appropriate to create trustworthy communication and brands by development of new products and services. It's all about creativity, innovation and design. We call it The Credibility Loop.

Before the line

You need an arsenal of hygiene factors just to be on the market nowadays. All competitors have good q uality, good service, good distribution, good person-nel, good price, good communication and good whatsoever...At Sony there is a saying that all products have the same function, performance, technology and price. The only thing that differentiates their products from their competitors is design. Why not putting most efforts in developing good design then?

There's lot of talking going on inside the creative industries concerning Above the Line (ATL) and Below the Line (BTL) communication. In the red corner sits ATL, which concerns traditional advertising in magazines, radio, TV and outdoor prints. In the blue corner we will find BTL, which concerns PR, web, DM, retail communication etc. If you ask us, ATL is knocked down. But we take the issue one step further and introduce our own BTL: Before the Line. Our BTL dances like a butterfly and stings like a bee...

Faster horses

Up to today the marketing people have been in charge for entering new products to the market, and this (only) because their job is to know what people like and want. But do they really know what people need? It's more interesting to see what people are doing instead of listening what they are saying. Look at your children; they do like you do, not like you tell them to do. And Henry Ford would probably got the answer "faster horses" instead of "a vehicle with a motor on four wheels" on a direct q uestion about peoples' needs.

We think the marketing people q uite often have the same narrow-minded thinking. A lot of them don't see beyond existing categories and often goes for what's already available and possible.

So, let a creative design culture sweep through the organisation and combine the innovative minds from the R&D department with the outgoing ditto from the marketing department. It is only by combining different skills and mindsets you can create real innovations that give you the possibility to change the future.

As you can't win the advertising battle - go for a ride with the Credibility Loop!

Let the products talk themselves. Give them a raison d'étre, personality and a soul! It's probably the best way to differentiate a product offer. And out of a strictly financial point of view: what are the reasons not produce products that communicate efficient itself?

Why not transfer money and efforts from the end (advertising) to the start (R&D) of a product life cycle? By doing this companies can be much more innovative and it will give them the possibility to build-in

communicative q ualities into the products from the start. And by giving products and services a better meaning, the chance is much greater that the target group will source them voluntarily.

A good example: When iPod was introduced year 2001 Apple spent 24,5 million dollars to launch the product. A huge amount of money, but still probably just a tenth of how much the cost would have been to reach the same global success with a less attractive product. Good design and word-of- mouth did most of the job.

Design = Economy as the great Swedish graphic designer Olle Eksell described it already back in 1964. Finally: It's all about taking charge of the situation.

A design strategy has its tentacles everywhere

We are certain that companies will build a much more credible brand with good design and innovation strategies instead of only wrapping up the products with ads in the end. The advertising money is much better used for innovations that makes a difference and that benefit both business and society. Who doesn't want to make peoples life better, more e q ual and hopefully happier by developing more attractive and sustainable products or services?

Some may argue that everything will be copied: product or service. Of course it will, if it's successful enough. When everybody has the same technology copies will always exist. So you have to differentiate and be uni q ue, you need to be smarter and pro-active. A good way forward is to be less technocratic and more pro-cultural, because the cultural values of a corporation are the most difficult part to blueprint by the copycats. By having an integrated design strategy within the corporate strategy (together with marketing, HR, R&D, finance etc.) you will come very far.

We are all familiar with the discussion from the eighties and forward about brands: "Our brand is our most valuable asset". Today it's common talks, and a hygiene factor. Nowadays the design strategy is the "new" brand strategy.

Successful companies with a clear design strategy like Apple have understood that the design issues must be discussed and decided at the highest management levels.

A design strategy should have its tentacles everywhere in a corporate strategy, that's why it's necessary and an unbeatable competitive advantage. It's beyond corporate identity and graphic design q uestions; it's about everything that happens in your company. How does your customer service respond, do you have fresh flowers and fruit in your office, what kind of music is played in the reception, is your logistics fully optimised, how is your product or service packed and how do you expose it? Everything counts, nothing is unimportant, you have to have holistic view and manage the process - the design process. It's your most important process, because design helps you to succeed with your communication. And with good communication you will reach out and become a happy and hopefully positive part of your costumers' minds.

To summarise the everlasting brand discussion: A brand and its value is the outcome of a design process.

Our windup

Today we all know that we have to develop, innovate and find new ways to survive - either it's business, personal or environmental concerns. At David Report we take our responsibility and focus on a business dilemma - why advertise when you can do something more powerful and actually both build your brand and sell more products/services by innovative R&D?

As you read above we argue for a shift from advertising into a design focused R&D. According to us this is the only way forward into tomorrow's society and business life. Design is also the best way to visualising your brand and your business strategy.

Be smart, q uestion the advertising standard and go for a ride in our credibility loop, or in other words: build your brand through a smart design strategy.

Arrays in C# .Net

What is an array?

In simplest terms, an array is an organized collection. It can be a collection of anything.

The important thing to remember is that it is a collection.

We use arrays every day

A pack of M&Ms is a great example of an array. It's easy for us to imagine a bag of this popular candy.

We can imagine each one of the M&Ms as they are taken from the bag. They are all basically the same but

different colors. Even though they are different colors, they are all chocolate candy with a hard candy

A bag of M&M's is an array of datatype M&M's. It is a collection of candy.

How do I declare an array?

Declaring an array is very much like declaring other variables. The only difference is that you are

declaring a variable that will hold more than one object. Let's compare these two declarations.

String strEmotion = "happy";

String[]strEmotions = {"happy","sad","elated","afraid","angry","peaceful"};

Both of the variables above, strEmotion and strEmotions, have been declared using Explicit Declaration which means the

value is set at the same time they are created.

By using the brackets [] , the compiler knows that the variable strEmotions will hold more than one value.

The number of items and the values is set with =

{"happy","sad","elated","afraid","angry","peaceful"};

In this case, we have set the size of the array to 6 because we have added 6 values.

How do I get a specific value?

Getting the value of each item isn't hard once you understand how the array refers to each item.

At first it might be a little confusing because arrays use a zero based reference.

This means that the first item in the list is in the 0 position. Huh?

Okay, look at the next lines and you'll understand.

String [] strEmotions = {"happy","sad","elated","afraid","angry","peaceful"};

strEmotions[0] = happy (Value in the 0 positon of the array)

strEmotions[1] = sad (Value in the 1 position of the array)

strEmotions[2] = elated (Value in the 2 position of the array)

strEmotions[3] = afraid (Value in the 3 position of the array)

strEmotions[4] = angry (Value in the 4 position of the array)

strEmotions[5] = peaceful (Value in the 5 position of the array)

Putting it all to work

In this example, we have an array of data type System.Drawing.Colors that we will use to change the background color of a form. This very simple application will help in understanding how to reference each of the different items in an array. It also shows how to find out which control called the function.

Let's look at each line...

First an array of data type System.Drawing.Color is declared and four colors, Green, Red, Yellow, and Blue are added at the same time.

Notice the brackets [] which signify an array declaration.

Because we populate the array at the time we declare it, we say that it was explicitly declared.

```
System.Drawing.Color[] myColorArray = {System.Drawing.Color.Green, System.Drawing.Color.Red ,
```

```
System.Drawing.Color.Yellow, System.Drawing.Color.Blue};
```

Now we add a method and assign it to the click event of all the radio buttons.

We could have written this under four different methods, one for each of the radio buttons.

But since they are almost identical, it's better to add them in one method and then find out which radio button called it.

This also makes it much easier to support later on down the road (One Method rather than Four Methods).

```
private void ChangeColors(object sender, EventArgs e)
```

```
{
```

```
/*Get a reference to the radio button that called the function.
```

We know that the control that is going to call this method will

be a Radio Button so first we create a variable of datatype Radio Button.

Then we set our variable = to the sender object.

But we need first to convert the sender variable to a datatype of Radio*/

System.Windows.Forms.RadioButton rbtn = (System.Windows.Forms.RadioButton)sender;

Next find out which radio button it was by finding the name of the button.

if (rbtn.Name == "rbtnGreen")

this.BackColor = myColorArray[0];//

JavaScript and Ajax

JavaScript is client side scripting language. When you open a web page your web browser first downloads all the necessary files from the server to display that page correctly. Those necessary files are HTML, CSS, Images, Videos, etc and the JavaScript files too. After completing download the browser displays that page on its window and any script linked with it will run from the downloaded script file.

In Ajax technology, user inputs and other data are sent to the web server through JavaScript. JavaScript creates XML_HTTP_REQUEST_OBJECT to connect with the server, submit data to it, and to re q uest a response from the server. When response comes, a JavaScript event fires and the function associated with that event is then executed. So in Ajax technology JavaScript is only used to transfer data between client side and the server side while the main program, i.e. data processing is executed at the server end, in PHP or any other server side language.

As JavaScript runs from the client computer its execution time is very short, almost instantaneous. Viewers can run JavaScript without being connected with the server as well. But in Ajax, viewers must be connected to the server. Here execution time is much longer which depends on their Internet connection speed, server hardware and number of bytes to be transferred between client side and server side.

In terms of server security JavaScript is absolutely safe since it doesn't transfer any user input from client side to the server. But in Ajax you have to take special care to prevent any malicious data from the bad users.

In JavaScript you can't hide your source code. Users can easily read your source code from source view which is running on their computer. But in Ajax data processing takes place at the server end and so user can't see the program source code.

In Ajax you can support your program with your server database.

For a long program, if you use JavaScript to implement it, the size of your web page will be larger. So it will take longer time to download which is a bad SEO feature. But in Ajax you can run long program, processing several thousands of data from a database, still your page size keeps small.

Since all browsers do not strictly follow any particular standard so it is not very easy to write a browser independent JavaScript program.

JavaScript are only used in some specific applications where data security is not an important consideration while the scope of Ajax technology application is unlimited.

CSS - The Basics

Thinking about CSS, but want to learn what you need to know, or need to learn before jumping onto the CSS bandwagon? Let me begin by saying that CSS can reduce your time at the computer. But knowledge do you need to learn and is CSS compatible with the search engines and your browsers?

These are some of the questions I'll try to answer,as well as, explain a little about what CSS is all about.

What is CSS?

CSS stands for Cascading Style Sheets. CSS is a set of formatting instructions that controls the looks of a web page or pages. Some of the browsers that support CSS is: (Firefox,IE3 or later, NN4 or later). You may be saying, great this will definitely save me some time. Not so fast, you also need to know that though, the majority of the browsers understand CSS, they do not fully support all of it's capabilities.

XHTML - XHTML is EXtensible HyperText Markup Language. XHTML Is HTML with stricter rules-that adds conformity and, is 100% XML compliant. So you should be familiar with or become more comfortable with HTML, XHTML, and the style properties of CSS.

What can you do with CSS

You can build your layout,adjusting size and color of your headings or body text, as well as positioning your pictures. This translates into like pages being programmed once, without the choice of inputting the same coding into each of your web pages manually. Translated, elimination of duplicate formatting.

How to get the Search Engines to See Your Copy

It has been said that the Search Engines still have some problems with understanding CSS. But if you want to use CSS, is there a way to get the search engines to see what you want.

1. Keep your text clean, if you have to much garbage in your web page, than the spiders will have a difficult time in determining what is relevant and what is not. Thus, CSS keeps your web page clean, without the redundant coding needed for each individual element of code. Here is an example of how to code a headline; with the CSS code below.

Example: "h1"Title"/h1" (replace beginning and end q uotes with)

"CSS code: H1 {font family: Arial size: 18 px; bold;}" (leave off q uotes)

Syntax of CSS

First, CSS can be written within any text editor. But the text file must be saved with a CSS extension.

The syntax of CSS consists of the selector and the declaration. The selector is the identifier within the body of your web page; the declaration is the code that identifies the style that you want to put into place as to property and rule. Lets say you want all your H1 headlines to be green, with the font Arial. the code for CSS would be as follows:

Note: Do not include q uotes around the code.

"selector {property: rule;}"

"H1 {color: green; font-family: Arial;}"

Note: Notice that the property and rule must be enclosed in {}.

Placement of CSS

There are three places to put your CSS code:

In the Head (Internal), in an external file, or within an individual tag (Inline style).

Internal -is used within a single web page that may have a uni q ue style.

Inline - mixes code with content. Sometimes you may need to use it, but this style does seem to eliminate the need of even using a CSS style sheet.

External - The CSS is separate from the body of the web page and is linked with the web page. Thus, to link an external file into a web page you will need to use the link tag.

Example:

<link rel="stylesheet" type="text/css" href="NameofCSS.css"> (Goes in the head section after the title tag)

Which way do you go? If you have a large site or a site that will be expanding, an external file would be a better way to q uickly and easily manipulate all your web pages at once.

Watch out for Spam

But with anything on the Internet, CSS can be used for the good and the bad. And obviously, if you want to keep your site up and running for a long time, some CSS techni q ues should be avoided. Why? Because some CSS

techni q ues can be considered spam by the search engines and thus, ban your site if you use the techni q ues. The blackhat tactics include such things as: 1) using CSS to hide text-from headlines to body from the human eye; 2) hiding and bolding or italicizing copy for search engine spiders benefit only.

To conclude, CSS can and is a viable way to making your web pages easier to maintain-if the majority of your pages follow the same format. If you are not all that familiar with CSS, then take the time to look at w3schools.com tutorial. It's very informative and can get you started with CSS..

Conclusion

JavaScript is a wonderful technology to use on the web. It is not that hard to learn and it is very versatile. It plays nicely with other web technologies such as HTML and CSS and can even interact with plugins such as Flash.

JavaScript allows us to build highly responsive user interfaces, prevent frustrating page reloads and even fix support issues for CSS. Using the right browser add-ons (such as Google Gears or Yahoo Browser Plus) you can even use JavaScript to make online systems available offline and sync automatically once the computer goes online.

JavaScript is also not restricted to browsers. The speed and small memory footprint of JavaScript in comparison to other languages brings up more and more uses for it from automating repetitive tasks in programs like Illustrator, up to using it as a server-side language with a standalone parser. The future is wide open; no matter what you do as a web developer in the nearer future, I am q uite sure you will have to work with JavaScript sooner or later. .....

Don't miss out!

Visit the website below and you can sign up to receive emails whenever Brian Evenson publishes a new book. There's no charge and no obligation.

https://books2read.com/r/B-A-RSXW-RTHGC

BOOKS 2 READ

Connecting independent readers to independent writers.

Also by Brian Evenson

Java Programming
Python Programming
JavaScript

About the Author

Called "one of the world's foremost authors of books about programming" by International Developer magazine, best-selling author Brian Evenson has written about programming for over three decades. His books have sold millions of copies worldwide and have been widely translated. Brian is interested in all facets of computing, but his primary focus is computer languages. He is the author of numerous books on Java, C, C++, Python etc. Brian holds BA and MCS degrees from the University of Illinois, Urbana/Champaign.